THE TALK

DATING, MARRIAGE, SEX, AND CHILDREN

THE TALK

DATING, MARRIAGE, SEX, AND CHILDREN

The godly guidance Christian parents should give to their children

THE DEACON

The Talk: Dating, Marriage, Sex, and Children

The godly guidance Christian parents should give to their children.

The Talk: Dating, Marriage, Sex, and Children
The godly guidance Christian parents should give to their children/ The Deacon – 1st ed.

ISBN 978-1-7366510-0-1 (Paperback)
ISBN 978-1-7366510-1-8 (eBook)

To Our Children

TABLE OF CONTENTS

PREFACE

Children come into puberty curious about sex, sexuality, and marriage. They are exposed to worldly concepts in the media and through others. Few kids see or hear the Godly answers to their questions. The reluctance of some parents to discuss sexual matters with their children or the parent's ignorance concerning God's direction on sex and marriage leave the young vulnerable.

The Talk is a solution to the problem of parents not being able to provide their children with Christian guidance on sexual matters. Whether parents shy from the subject or just don't know the Christian answers, The Talk meets the need. It saves them from having to search through the scriptures for many of their answers. It is recommended the parent and child read and discuss the book together. But, if the parent lacks the courage to do that, they can simply offer their child this book and when they find the courage, discuss the book with them. In any case, the children should not go into the world unarmed.

The Talk can be called a self-help book for young and new Christians wanting to live a life pleasing unto God. It addresses an area of life that can be most damaging. There are many who now look at their lives, especially those who have taken on the burden of single parenthood, who wish they had first read a book like this.

The table of contents is your guide for important questions concerning dating, marriage, sex, and children. Simply scan the table to find the question(s) you are interested in, then go to the referenced page for your answer.

INTRODUCTION

Parents, when your children come to that social age when they begin thinking about dating and sex, you must be prepared to have "The Talk." It is time to tell that child about dating, marriage, sex, and children. This is an awesome responsibility, especially in the church, because if you don't teach them God's way, the world will teach them its way. The first question is, do you accept God's way? You may note that this introduction is aimed at the parents and not the children. That is because parents must make the decision as to whether or not this book will be used by them or given to their child. The next question is, do you know God's way?

A young boy confesses to his dad that he had sex with a girl. The dad's chest swells with pride at the idea that his boy is now a man. A young girl is sitting next to her mother and asks, "Momma, when will I know?" Her daughter wonders when she'll know it is time to have sex. Mom replies, "When the time is right, you'll know." She smiles, satisfied that she has given her daughter good advice, believing girls have an intuition about such things. But are these the responses of Christian parents? Do you know what the Christian responses should be?

This book provides godly answers. At the foundation of it is the godly order of things, which in these times would be attraction, dating (in western culture), marriage, and then sex. And, knowing this order, the father in the example above should have warned, "Son, that's not the way. God wants you to marry first." That mother should have said, "The time is right after you've taken your wedding vows. And the right man to lose your virginity to is your husband."

Of course, in modern society, the idea of preserving one's virginity is treated like foolishness or something that is undoable. We treat those who demand their children respect God's call to virginity as oppressors when such a demand is good in the eyes of God and for mankind. And you, parent, may have been one of those who railed against God's way. Woe to those who call good evil (Isaiah 5:20).

In the western media, we see couples jump from attraction to the bedroom. And society follows the same pattern. The 'one-night stand' or 'hookup' is now common. And sex is treated as a requirement for dating. Where is marriage? Marriage is rarely in the picture. And when it is, it is of low priority. Most Christians know that all sexual activity outside of marriage is a sin to God, yet they follow the way of the world. They not only have sex outside of marriage but encourage others to do the same (Romans 1:32). How often do we make jokes about 'getting some?' We ignore the many ills of society that can be connected to the collapse of the family and sex outside of marriage. Knowledgeable Christians consider this Satan's attack on God's institution of marriage.

How many criminals are children born out of wedlock? How many impoverished families are single-parent families – not because a parent died, but because they were the product of a "hookup?"

With all the problems that sex outside of marriage will cause our children, they are driven to have sex at an earlier and earlier age. A significant number of preteens are now sexually active. Why is that? Why do they lose their innocence so young? It is because society has surrounded them with corrupt ideas and images that encourage the behavior. That includes the actions of friends and relatives. Some of it is so common we don't even pay attention to it.

At one time in our culture, movies and TV shows were censored for the express purpose of keeping children relatively innocent until they were old enough for the subject of sex. Censorship also promoted Christian values. It was understood that just seeing or hearing about something might make a child want to explore it. This is especially true of sex and sexuality. However, God does not require perfect innocence. What he does require is that our children know his laws concerning these things, and it is the parents who should teach the social and spiritual consequences of having sex outside of marriage. Unfortunately, our children see something sexual almost every day without it being in the appropriate order. In fact, it is the sinful order that is glorified – from strangers becoming lovers in a movie to strangers getting turned on in a jean commercial. Aggressive slam-against-the-wall sex is now cliché. And marriage is not included in the order of things.

It is bad enough that some children will lose their innocence to some adult molester. In this sex-charged world, molestation is becoming more common. However, the majority of children will lose their innocence to a form of immoral indoctrination. Where children once had to imagine sex, they can now see it in the love scenes on our television and movie screens, the booty-shaking videos, the lyrics in music, and graphic images of magazines. And, that behavior is reinforced by the people around them at various, unlikely sources.

A hair commercial comes on, and the woman in the commercial is moaning, just like the woman in that movie sex scene they saw. What comes to the mind of the child? A man in a commercial is driving an awesome car, and he exchanges lustful looks with a provocatively dressed woman passing on the street. What are the kids thinking? Are our boys thinking a fine car can make you sexy? Are our girls thinking they should surrender themselves to the guy with the fine car? We don't have to guess. That is the subliminal intent of the commercials.

A mother brings her child into the store and passes a magazine rack full of magazines showing women in thong bikinis, bodies gleaming with oil. The cover girls seem to be looking seductively at the child – their bulging body parts on provocative display. What do you think is going on in the child's head? Does the little girl think she should aspire to look like those women? Does the little boy think those are the kind of women he should pursue?

Dance videos show our kids that if they want to be one of the hot kids, they have to hump and grind against others as they dance. They show the girls if they want to be one of the hot chicks, they have to show lots of body and gyrate like a stripper. And to see those gyrations, one need look no further than school dance or at the cheerleaders who perform acrobatics less and shake booty more. And the humping, gyrating, twerking cheers are taught by adult women to elementary school children. What are they thinking? And while the girls are learning to be provocative, boys are learning that real men must be demanding – telling girls what they want in graphic terms and groping them to let the level of their interest be known. With all of these things pressing on them, children are in a rush to experience sex. What is worse, they fully expect to experience it outside of marriage.

At one time in our history, a big deal was made of the wedding night and the loss of virginity ON THAT NIGHT. Virginity was considered a girl's special dowry. Society worked to aid girls in keeping their virginity, and even in movies, preserving virginity was a big deal. It was generally understood that boys wanted to marry virgins. The world now teaches that reaching adulthood as a virgin is backwards. Where in the past, children acted in ways that would preserve them, now they act in ways that will hasten the day of them becoming sexually active.

There is a spiritual battle about sex that many kids find too spooky to talk about. The truth is that Satan is the prince of this world (Ephesians 2:2). And it is he that influences a culture in which obeying God is treated as wrong. Note how quickly Christians are attacked for daring to lay down moral rules for their children. Yet all manners of corrupting influences are allowed for those same children. Think about it; indoctrinating children into morality is treated as wrong while indoctrinating them into sinfulness is not. Again, "Woe to those who treat good as evil." (Isaiah 5:20).

This book, The Talk, recognizes that God is an all-knowing God. He knew what was best for us when He laid down his laws about sex and marriage. For example, don't you think God knew that if mankind could have sex without commitment, that's what they'd do? Thus, He made marriage the first requirement. Now, it is common for a couple to live together and have children without ever marrying. It is also common for one of the partners to just walk away from the relationship and deal a crushing blow to their mate and children. It is then that one learns that what they thought would lead to marriage was just a convenience for one of them. Old expressions like "Why buy the cow when the milk is free?" suddenly make sense. God's apparent purpose in requiring marriage before sex is to prevent these and other painful deceptions, as well as to provide stable homes for children.

So, how did mankind get into this mess with relationships? We aren't looking for what God wants us to have – godly spouses. Our goals shape our attractions. What is your goal in dating? Are you looking for a hot escort and satisfying sex partner or a godly person to marry? The former will lead you to put the cart before the horse, that is, have sex outside of marriage. Rather than seek a hard-working provider, girls go for the sexually exciting bad boys. And instead of boys looking for wives and mothers, they are looking for sex freaks. It is only when that bad boy and sex freak refuse to change that the warning, "Don't marry a project, marry what you want," hits home.

Here is the truth: God's laws about sex were the best thing for us in the beginning, and they are the best thing for us now. He established his rules, knowing the effect of them through all of time. Why would we think He'd make any rule that would expire? And since we can't see into the future as God can, what makes us think we can create any rules that would render His obsolete?

We often say that the Lord is the same yesterday, today, and forevermore (Hebrews 13:8). Well, this is true of men, too, because while technology changes and places change, the nature of mankind does not. And God's rules concerning sex are based on His knowledge of our nature. If you consider yourself a god-fearing Christian, you want your children to grow up knowing the godly rules concerning sex and marriage. The problem is that you may not know them nor have the patience to scour the scriptures for them. "The Talk" seeks to help you in this regard.

In this book, we will give the godly responses to a number of questions youth might have as they enter into puberty and dating. In some of these responses, this book may show the difference between worldly and godly thinking about dating, marriage, sex, and children. Just go to the table of questions and see if your question is there. Then go to the page indicated to receive the godly answer. The godly answers are scripture-based and will show you what God desires. When the socially accepted responses are given, you may note that they run counter to what God wants you to do. Don't be surprised. Jesus himself says that Satan is the prince of the world (John 16:11), and Satan has sought to get us to defy God's laws since the beginning (Genesis 3). It stands to reason that Satan would sponsor ideas that defy God. With "The Talk" in hand, you now have a choice between following Satan and following God concerning love, marriage, sex, and children. Why do you have a choice? You have a choice because you will know both sides. Know the difference between eternal damnation and eternal life. Choose life.

A final warning. Satan now has the most powerful medium for corrupting our children - the internet. It will show them every possible sin. And it will often put those sins in a context that makes them seem all right, even normal. What is worse, your child may be searching for something innocent and have something pornographic pop-up, then curiosity will cause your child to look at it. Be warned.

PART 1
DATING

This section offers godly guidance on dating and also touches on the subject of attraction.

THE PURPOSE OF DATING

1. What is God's guidance on dating?

Answer: God provides no rules concerning dating. Most marriages in scripture were arranged. The courtship was part of the marriage agreement. However, God did let us know what we should be looking for by the laws he wrote. In a nutshell, we should be seeking virgins who know and respect the marriage institution and are prepared to establish a proper home. The details of that will be given in response to other questions.

2. What would God's reason be for me dating?

Answer: God's only reason for you to date would be to find a suitable spouse. By the way, that does not include sexual test runs. Sex is reserved for the married.

3. Who should initiate dating?

Answer: It should always be the man. Scripture refers to a man finding a good wife (Proverbs 18:22). There is no reference to women finding a husband. Plus, it seems that if the man must invest in a woman, he will love and value her all the more, such as with Jacob and Rachel (Genesis 29). Jacob worked 14 years for Rachel and loved her so much. And how often has life shown us that when the women hunt for men, the men lose respect for them? They never marry them, cheat or divorce early.

4   What would God's objection be to me dating?

Answer: If you demonstrate a lack of moral discipline. If you expect to have sex in the dating, you're not spiritually mature enough to date. If you are creating habits that will be destructive to marriage, you're not spiritually mature enough to date. For example, if you grow accustomed to dating more than one person at a time, you aren't developing the discipline to be faithful to one person (Read Hosea and ask why Gomer was driven to cheat on a godly man).

5   What should I do before beginning to date?

Answer: Begin by praying that God will send you someone. When the servant of Abraham was told to find a mate for Abraham's son, Isaac, the servant prayed to God for help and asked that the woman do a certain thing to indicate she was the one. Whether you are male or female, ask God to send you someone and then patiently wait for them.

6   Where should I look for someone I'd like to date?

Answer: You might meet a good prospect anywhere – store, home gatherings, church, etc. However, the more decadent the setting, the less likely you'll find good prospects. The people at a gathering tend to share similar views. Look for a place frequented by people of good character.

7   Who should I hang out with to find a date?

Answer: Hang out with people of good character – preferably Christians. Psalms 1 provides the first evidence that one is of good, even godly character. They don't hang around or listen to people who are worldly and mock God.

8   What is the danger of hanging with the bad group?

Answer: Scripture says that if you keep bad company, it will corrupt your character (1 Corinthians 15:33). People who hang out with an immoral and rowdy crowd are expected to act the same in order to fit in. We know it as peer pressure.

9   What is the benefit of hanging with the nice crowd?

Answer: If you hang out with a moral or 'nice' crowd, they will expect you to act in good character. Those friends will prove a blessing to you by steering you in a godly direction (Psalms 1:1). It is also among the nice crowd that nice people look for companions.

10   What kind of people should I date?

Answer: Date people with good reputations (Psalm 1) and someone who embodies what you asked God for. You asked for them. Be looking for them.

11   What if I just want to date someone who looks hot?

Answer: Pray that they are also people of good character (Proverbs 11:22). Many wives in scripture are identified as both godly and beautiful. Genesis 29:17 describes Jacob's wife, Rachel, as pretty and shapely. You could say she was all that.

12 What if I'm approached by someone who is too nice?

Answer: If you think they are too nice, you may not be mature enough for them. We often reject people who act with morals, seeing respect and responsibility as corny, lame, or weak. We pass them over because they don't bring worldly excitement. And, in our youth, sexual excitement is very important as it makes us feel desirable (1 John 2:16). However, if you can respect them enough to learn something about them, you might discover they are the one that God sent you.

13 So, what do I lose if I pass over the 'too nice' person?

Answer: You may be losing the best choice for you. As we mature, the excitement of youth becomes less important than having a mature partner. Later, we may realize that the 'too nice' person was the right person. You might think, "Gee, I wish I had married them instead of what's his/her face!"

14 What if I simply don't want someone who is 'too nice?'

Answer: We don't usually respect people we label as 'too nice.' So, don't date them; you'll just abuse them. No one deserves that. Wait until you are spiritually able to respect people of good character.

15 What if I prefer the bad boys/girls?

Answer: You're not spiritually mature. God tells us to flee from our youthful lusts, and that is what the bad boys and girls represent – our youthful lust. They stand for drama, challenge, adrenaline rush, and sexual excitement. And they keep us living with sinful temptations.

16 What if the bad one is charming and really looks good?

Answer: Be patient. God can send you a good-looking, charming, and godly person or change the bad person for your sake. Abraham's wife Sarah was so gorgeous that the Pharaoh of Egypt wanted her for his harem even though she was well up in years (Genesis 12:10-20). However, the Apostle Peter mentioned her as an example of inner beauty (1 Peter 3:1-6).

17 What's wrong with looking for a good-looking, charming person?

Answer: Nothing. However, you can be deceived by charm and looks fade, but the godly person is a treasure (Proverbs 31:30). While seeking someone with charm and looks, also search for character.

18 I'm a Christian. Should I date only Christians?

Answer: That would be the smartest thing to do if you want a Christian spouse, but it is not commanded. God tells us, through the Apostle Paul, it could be a bad thing for a Christian to marry a non-Christian (2 Corinthians 6:14). However, it is not beyond God to send you someone so that you can bring them to Christ. That doesn't mean you go after someone expecting to change them. Don't choose a project; choose a spouse.

19   What if the one I really like is not a Christian?

Answer: You take your chances with the non-Christian. This is especially true when you reach the point of considering marriage (Read what happened to Samson in Judges 13 thru 16). Again, that doesn't mean that this person was not for you. Just as you were once not a Christian and were saved, perhaps God will save this person through you. But be careful. The greatest danger is that they pull you away from God.

20   What if I've dated and fallen in love with a non-Christian?

Answer: Pray and hold to your faith. If you date or marry an unbeliever, God may save them through you (1 Corinthians 7:16). If they turn toward God, then God has worked it out for you. If it becomes obvious you're dating someone who is just playing you along in hopes of a sexual relationship, find the strength to break it off (Proverbs 4:23). It will hurt, but God will comfort you (2 Corinthians 1:3-4).

21   How do I keep from attracting the wrong kind?

Answer: You can't. The scriptures suggest you dress modestly and that you emphasize good behavior (1 Timothy 2:9, 10). Understand that acting and dressing like a good person will maximize your ability to attract good people but won't ward off the bad ones, especially if you are naturally attractive. In fact, they may see corrupting you [taking your virginity, for instance] as a challenge.

22 What do I do if an undesirable person latches onto me?

Answer: Let them know that they can't corrupt or use you. Except for the stalker and criminally minded, the undesirable will move on when they realize there is nothing in it for them (James 4:7).

23 What's wrong with just looking for a hookup?

Answer: If by 'hookup' you mean just-for-sex, it is a sin in the eyes of God. When the Bible uses the word 'fornication,' it is talking about hooking up – two unmarried people having sex. Sadly, the 'hookup' is replacing the first kiss in western culture. And, that makes sense if you understand that Satan is doomed, and he knows you will be doomed with him if you are a fornicator (1 Corinthians 6:9).

24 Can't you hookup while single and then repent when you're married?

Answer: Yes. You can repent of any sin. And marriage can be seen as an act of repentance for those couples engaged in fornication. Play it safe. Pray God's forgiveness for previous sins.

25 What effect can having a few sex partners have on me?

Answer: Aside from subjecting you to disease and unwanted pregnancy, it can make being true to one person difficult. You do what you're accustomed to (Jeremiah 13:23). When you are accustomed to having sex with multiple partners, you learn to put one partner out of your mind when you're with the other. Having multiple partners is practice for adultery.

SAFEGUARDS IN DATING

1   How do I guard against my own sexual feelings when dating?

Answer: If you were honest enough to ask this question, you have taken the first step in preventing sexual sin – admitting your weakness. There are several things you can do. Most of them are common sense application of God's command to flee from sin (1 Corinthians 6:18, 10:14, 2 Timothy 2:22):

1. **Keep in mind that God sees all that you do.** In the back, in the corner, in the dark, God sees it all (Psalms 139). Keep that in mind, and you may avoid doing wrong.

2. **Avoid seductive situations.** You know the plan – darkly lit place, sexy music, lots of alcohol. All of that is designed to seduce you. The idea is to draw you by your own lust (James 1:14).

3. **Avoid seductive dancing.** This means dancing with excessive body contact or moving too seductively. Contrary to the song 'Bump and Grind,' there is something wrong with it. *In some past cultures, dancing between unmarried males and females was forbidden.*

4. **Especially avoid sexual touching** - feeling each other up/petting. Petting builds up your desire to a fever pitch and makes resisting your desire near impossible.

5. **Don't get caught up in sex talk.** When the serpent approached Eve, he talked about the forbidden fruit (Genesis 3). And, in the end, Eve took a bite of the forbidden fruit. The person talking sex to you is using Satan's (the serpent's) ploy. They want you to take a bite.

6. **Avoid intimate situations with people who sexually excite you.** Knowing the danger of intimate situations, many old-world cultures chaperoned the unmarried through their courtships. And that is good advice today. The chaperone does not have to be in the party, but near enough that they can walk in at any time. This is a natural deterrent to bad behavior. When friends say come because my parents are out, don't come.

7. **Before you have sex, think of the consequences.** You can catch a disease. You can become a single parent. And, especially in the case of girls, you can spoil yourself for marriage – loss of virginity, loss of self-esteem, loss of self-discipline, and skeletons (secrets) in your closet.

Remember, the person trying to get you in the bed is already there in their own mind. They're trying to get you excited enough to join them. And that's what you must guard against your own lust rising. The three-part attack has been the same since the time of Adam. We lust after things because of how they look, feel/taste to us, or make us feel about ourselves. Or as 1 John 2:16 (KJV) puts it, "...the lust of the flesh, and the lust of the eyes and the pride of life." The serpent showed Eve the forbidden fruit "...was good for food and pleasing to the eye, and also desirable for gaining knowledge ..." (Genesis 3:6). So, expect the sexual seduction to include promises that it will feel good; questions like, "Don't you like me?" and promises it will make a man or woman of you.

2   What kind of places should I go to on a date?

Answer: Go to places that offer maximum fun with minimum temptation. Teens should go to parties that have responsible adults nearby. There should be no concern about what the adults will see when they peek in on the party. Especially avoid places where alcohol and drug use are being pushed (Proverbs 20:1), and there will be no adults around. If you watch many movies, the club scene with drugs, alcohol, and raunchy dancing is promoted. Others show wild parties taking place when the parents are away. Such movies even show how people are taken advantage of when drunk or high at such places. These movies are fiction based on fact. Common sense says you should avoid such scenes.

3   How do I avoid encouraging sinful lust?

Answer: Be honest with yourself. If you choose your clothing because it looks sexy, admit that, and dress it down.   When you dance seductively, you know you want those looking at you to be excited – admit that, and tone it down. Plus, don't be a seductive flirt. However, when you've done all that you can to minimize lust, people may still lust after you. The book of Esther shows that it is not always a bad thing.

4   Why do we tease?

Answer: We tease for attention and validation. We want to know we have the power of seduction.   That falls under the heading, "boasting." (1 John 1:16).

5   What are the consequences of teasing?

Answer: It can attract wanted and unwanted attention. Now, if wanted attention leads to consensual sex, it is still fornication unless you are married. If you make someone stumble, you are as responsible for their sin as for yours (Luke 17:1, 2). It also can make one vulnerable to the crime of rape. The attractive face may hide a criminal mind.

6 You mean I can't be attractive – even sexy?

Answer: Of course, you can be attractive. God blessed you with that. Just be attractive and not whorish. And what's the difference? Whorish is presenting yourself in a way that is intended to cause others to lust after you. A Christian's attractiveness should include spiritual attractiveness (1 Timothy 2:9, 10. 1 Peter 3:3-6).

7 Can I drink alcohol on a date?

Answer: Drink alcohol only in moderation and if you are of legal age. Remember, alcohol and drugs are often used to weaken someone so that they will do things they know are wrong (Proverbs 20:1). And that has been true since the beginning of time. Lot's daughters were able to commit incest with their father by first getting him drunk (Genesis 19:30-33).

8 How do I know if the person I'm with is trying to have sex with me?

Answer: This seems like a silly question, but some people haven't learned what subtle sexual aggression looks like. The answer is if they are saying words that will make you feel sexual – compliments on your figure and on how desirable you are (Proverbs 6:24) as they try to entice you with their eyes (Proverbs 6:25), they're thinking sex. The words may be innocent, but the effect is not.

9   Is it such a bad thing to think about having sex with someone?

Answer: First of all, it is a common occurrence. However, Jesus said, "But I tell you that anyone who looks at a woman lustfully has already committed adultery with her in his heart." (Matthew 5:28). The same is true of all sexual thoughts. The first step toward doing it is thinking about it.

10   How can I tell if my date is looking for a spouse and not just a sex partner?

Answer: You can't be sure until the marriage. However, there is a simple test: make it clear there will be no sex before marriage. If they drop you like a hot potato, sex was their primary goal. As the scripture says, "Resist the devil, and he will flee." (James 4:7). If they are fine with you saving yourself for marriage, they want to know you, and such a person might be a good prospect.

11   Must my date meet my parents?

Answer: Always. Parents (even the not-so-good ones) are one of your best safeguards. Had Samson listened to his parents (Judges 14:3), he might not have been betrayed by a Philistine wife. Of course, God used that disobedience to bring about the overthrow of the Philistines (Judges 14:4).

12   When must my date meet my parents?

Answer: Before the first date. Secret relationships can negatively affect your relationship with your parents. You may act aggressively toward them as you try to hide your secret friend. Your parents will have no clues as to where this behavior is coming from. Also, they cannot advise you about a relationship they don't know about. There is a saying: "If the ship leaves without the captain, he can't help when it starts to sink." That's one of those old folk sayings.

13 What advantage is there in introducing my date to my parents?

Answer: Parents are more capable of noting your date's shortcomings, while you might be blinded to them by your emotions. We tend to overlook the obvious faults of those to whom we are attracted because we want to be with them. Parents want to protect us, so they have a more critical eye. Whether you think your parents have it right or not, at least hear what they have to say. You might gain a new understanding of the person you're dating (Proverbs 1:8, 4:1).

14 What if my date would rather not meet my parents?

Answer: Don't date that person. People prefer to do their dirt in secret. Scripture uses the expression "darkness" as in "out of the light" – because people don't want to be observed as they do their dirt (John 3:19, 20). There is no good reason why someone would want to have a close relationship with you while remaining anonymous to your parents.

15 What if I don't want my date to meet my parents?

Answer: This usually means you are trying to deny your parents an opportunity to assess your choice. God expects you to obey your parents in everything (Colossians 3:20). Hiding your relationships is an attempt to deny them the opportunity to be parents. You are rebelling against them and God.

16   What if my parents are overly protective of me with my date?

Answer: If your parents are overly protective, your reluctance is understandable. Sit down with your parents and prepare the way for them to meet this person. Come to some agreement about how they will treat your date. Most of all, give them the assurance that YOU won't be corrupted by your date. God wants you to obey your parents (Colossians 3:30). That is a lot easier if you understand each other.

17   What if my parents don't trust anyone I date?

Answer: Don't be surprised if their concern is not your love interest but you. Your parents may have seen exploitable weaknesses in you. Let them talk to you about those weaknesses before getting into a relationship (Proverbs 4:1). And, be prepared to hear that the dates you choose are the kind who will exploit your weaknesses. For example, girls from an abusive home may tend to pick abusive men.

18   Why should I obey my parents concerning my choice of dates?

Answer: First, because God required it (Exodus 20:12, Ephesians 6:1, Colossians 3:2). God works through our parents for our good. Our disobedience usually works out badly for us. In fact, God makes the point that obedience to your parents can lengthen your life (Ephesians 6:1-3). Pay attention to them. Even the not-so-good parents can give guidance that makes a lot of sense.

19   How should I dress for a date?

Answer: Modestly. God shows us through examples in scripture that people DO judge you by how you dress (Genesis 38:13-18, Judges 16:1 and Proverbs 7:10). How you dress suggests what type of person you are. *An old folks saying: "Girls who show their goodies to many will give their goodies to many."* Such old sayings seek to connect the way we dress with our attitude.

20 How do I know if I'm dressed too provocatively?

Answer: The rule is simple: If it over-emphasizes your body, it's too provocative. Women especially should dress modestly (1 Timothy 2:9). The question, of course, is what is modest? That has changed over the centuries. However, no matter how loose or conservative the times, we know when we are emphasizing our bodies. The choice of clothing is a conscious thing and if all the people around you can see is how "sexy" you look, you're dressing too provocatively.

21 Is it my fault if the way I dress excites someone?

Answer: Yes, especially if you purposely dressed to be provocative. Some of us look provocative, no matter what we wear, and know that if we don't dress it down, we'll excite someone. And we will be held accountable for their sinful thoughts and desires (Luke 17:1-2).

22 Can't I dress sexy if I want to?

Answer: Yes. God won't force you to obey him. You have free will. However, expect there to be consequences (Romans 13:2).

23 What's wrong with being physically attractive to another?

Answer: Nothing. It is God's blessing, and He may have given it to you to bring you to a special place. The Bible is full of attractive people whose good looks served God. Joseph was so handsome that the wife of his Egyptian master tried to force him to have sex with her (Genesis 39:7). She lied on him, and he was imprisoned for attempted rape, but God used contacts in the prison to elevate Joseph to save both Egypt and neighboring countries from starvation in a terrible famine. The beautiful Esther became Queen of Persia after winning a beauty contest and from that position was able to save her people from extermination (Book of Esther). As her uncle, Mordecai, said, "And who knows but that you have come to royal position for such a time as this?"

24 How does God expect me to use my good looks?

Answer: To attract a mate and open doors. Scripture is full of instances where attractiveness drew people together, such as Jacob and Rachel (Genesis 29:10-17). Rachel was described as lovely in form and beautiful (Genesis 29:17). Of course, it opened doors in different ways for Joseph and Esther.

25 What is the appropriate way to be attractive?

Answer: Let your beauty shine from within (Read 1 Peter 3:3, 4i). A beautiful spirit is an "unfading beauty." You will run into old and wrinkled people who come across as beautiful because of that inner spirit. The nice figure and smooth skin won't be with you always. You may meet beautiful people who have hardness that make them unattractive. You may meet attractive people who are proud and look down on others. God does not like such pride (Proverbs 16:5, 21:24, James 4:6). Don't be one of those ugly on the inside people.

26 When is my attractiveness a problem?

Answer: Attractiveness is a problem when it causes others to lust (Remember Joseph and the Egyptian master's wife). If you have a desperate need for attention or validation, you may use your attractiveness in the wrong way. It may also become a problem because of the sinful people around you. So, be alert to what kind of people are around you.

27 Will God punish me for being provocative?

Answer: Depends. God holds us accountable when we purposely cause others to fall (Proverbs 28:10. See King Jeroboam's fate after he caused Israel to fall in 1 Kings 15:29-30). That lady with the plunging neckline might feel she had done a good thing by reporting the unwanted approach of someone excited by it. But, before God, the question is, did she choose that plunging neckline to be provocative? (Matthew 18:6, 7).

28 Where can I dress provocatively?

Answer: Christians should not dress provocatively anywhere but before their spouses. We are always accountable to God for the sins we inspire, but provoking your spouse sexually is not sin (Read Song of Solomon).

29 What if I don't realize my outfit is too sexy?

Answer: If you bought an outfit because it displays your sexy body parts just right, you know the outfit is sexy. However, if you are one of those who look sexy in anything, ask someone to tell you if your outfit is too sexy. What's plain on one person might be provocative on another.

30 Shouldn't real Christians be able to ignore my sexiness?

Answer: NO! Saying things like, "If they were real Christians, they would not be looking at me like that," is total foolishness. It only shows that you don't know what a real Christian is. Being saved is not the same as being neutered. Your natural attractions don't go away. The spirit of God allows Christians to resist temptation (1 Corinthians 10:1), but they ARE tempted. A Christian is saved in spirit. They remain in the same lustful flesh. Only, they now have the Holy Spirit to help them control their flesh.

31   If you've got it, shouldn't you flaunt it?

Answer: No. That's a sex revolution phrase heard in the movie, *The Producers (1968)*. In the sexual 70s, it was justification for women wearing hot pants and micro-mini skirts and men wearing open-chested shirts and tight pants. Remember, there is a price for causing someone to sin. Beauty without discretion is like jewelry on a pig (Proverbs 11:22). Be discreet and humble in all your choices. It will make you appear more attractive and save you from unwanted attention and God's punishment for causing others to sin.

32   What if I attract others by showing that I have wealth?

Answer: This is never a good idea. If they come to you because of what you have, they can leave you because someone else has more (Proverbs 11:28). They may also leave you because they actually got to know someone else. They may not get to know you because they are too focused on what you have (1 Timothy 6:9, 10). Who you are is unique and everlasting. Emphasize who you are and don't try to buy affection and companionship with things. The most attractive thing you can display is virtue (Proverbs 31:10). A virtuous person is someone who is morally and ethically excellent.

33   Who are the safest dates?

Answer: The individual often called "too nice." These are the ones who won't press you to do anything wrong and try to prevent you from doing wrong because they care for you (Romans 13:10). If you are not spiritual, you may classify them as too nice. What they are is morally strong.

34 How will I recognize the "nice" prospect?

Answer: If you are still worldly, you might totally overlook them. If, however, you are maturing as a Christian, you will notice that the "nice" people focus on what's really important – getting to know you. They take joy in being with you, whether you have little or much to offer (Philippians 4:11).

35 How will I recognize the "worldly" prospect?

Answer: They want worldly things and don't understand you if you don't want the same things. Christian ideas like preserving yourself for marriage, not getting intoxicated, and not defiling your body are foolishness to them (1 Corinthians 2:14). Moreover, they build their worth on worldly things. For example, the girl who builds her worth on her sexiness can't respect the fellow who won't press her for sex. Such people won't entertain someone they consider "too nice."

36 What's the safest way to date?

Answer: Date in groups with people who know God and respect each other (Psalm 1:1).

37 What are good places for group dates?

Answer: The majority of entertainment places are OK – movies, restaurants, carnivals, dances, etc. However, all can be corrupted by alcohol, drugs, and sexual atmosphere. Avoid corrupted places.

38   What type of group dates should I avoid?

Answer: Those that promote sinful behavior – alcohol abuse, seductive dance, and the like. Unmarried teens should avoid any gatherings that are promoted as unchaperoned. The absence of chaperones is only important if they plan to do things they wouldn't want a chaperone to see. It is the reason John 3:19 says that men love darkness rather than light – "Because their deeds are evil."

39   Can Christians attend parties and dances?

Answer: Yes. Surprised? It depends on the atmosphere of the dance or party and their self-discipline. For instance, if there is heavy drug smoking, leave the party. A contact high is still a high. Now, with respect to enjoying music and friends, even if others are doing wrong, the Christians can choose just to enjoy the music and fellowship of like-minded friends. Jesus knows we must exist in this world and prayed that we'd be protected from the evil in the world (John 17:15-16). Consider this – sinners are in the world. How can you be a positive influence for them if you're never around them?

40   What should Christians avoid at a party or dance?

Answer: Avoid abuse of alcohol (if legal age) and drugs that might cloud your judgment (Proverbs 20:1); sexually exciting dances (pressing bodies); sexually suggestive talk, including song lyrics (2 Peter 2:18, Proverbs 7); intimate situations such as touching in dark corners. That leaves a lot of other things you can enjoy. Of course, if you are worldly, the things you should avoid may be what you were looking for.

41 What can Christians do at a party or dance?

Answer: Enjoy non-alcoholic beverages, food, fun conversation, line-dancing, partner dancing, and meet new people. If of legal drinking age, enjoy a modest drink of wine. The wine is not a sin. Overindulgence can lead to sin. Consider this: Jesus engaged in much of that – yet, did not sin. The wedding party where he turned the water into wine was a weeklong affair with dancing and socializing (John 2:1-11).

42 What is the most important safety precaution when dating?

Answer: Guard your heart (Proverbs 4:23). The proverb is not saying you should not fall in love. This is about not letting your affection control you. Some will say I love you to have sex with you, knowing that if they can capture your heart, they can lead you into sin. Don't let the serpent seduce you.

NOW THAT I'M DATING

1 What if I will lose my partner if I don't have sex with them?

Answer: Lose your partner. God tells us to flee sexual immorality (1 Corinthians 2:18). If they will leave you for not putting out, what's to keep them from leaving AFTER you've put out? Nothing. Many have come to realize in a painful way that it was never about them; it was about the sex. Once they gave that up, the sweet talk stopped, the phone calls stopped, and the pursuer moved on. This is nothing new. Read the story of Amnon and Tamar (2 Samuel 13). Amnon talked of loving Tamar, but after raping her, his love turned to intense hate. Why? It was lust all along. She had suggested they be married, but he dismissed that idea. It was all about the sex, and we still have to guard against people like Amnon.

2 Doesn't wanting to have sex with me mean they love me?

Answer: No. The only thing it clearly means is that they want to have sex with you. They might love you, but sometimes even they don't know if it is love or lust until after the sex. Then, when the thrill is gone, they leave. They may justify themselves by saying: "I love you, but I'm not IN love with you." That basically means they care enough not to want to hurt you, but the thrill is gone. Again, read the story of Amnon and Tamar to see how lust was mistaken for love (2 Samuel 13:1-19). These old Bible stories are examples for us to learn from. Man has not changed. We still confuse lust and love.

By the way, did you know that choosing to have sex outside of marriage to keep someone is an act of idolatry? That person is now more valuable to you than God. God requires us to flee from idolatry (1Corinthians 10:14).

3 Can sex break up a relationship?

Answer: Yes, especially for girls. Boys often test the strength of a girl's character by pressuring her for sex. The girl who doesn't give in passes the test. The girl that gives in shows that she can be pressured into doing wrong. And if she'll do wrong with him, she'll do wrong with someone else. Thus, he immediately loses trust in her because she did not protect her virtue (Proverbs 31:10, 11).

4 Shouldn't I have sex with someone to see if we're sexually compatible?

Answer: No. That's an excuse for sexual sinning. Satan is slick (Genesis 3:1). Searching for that perfect sexual fit can keep you in sin through dozens of partners.

5 Isn't having sex an expression of freedom?

Answer: In marriage, sex is an enjoyment you are free to have. Sex is addictive and was intended to bond you to your spouse. However, outside of marriage, it is an expression of your free will to choose between godliness and sin. And it will enslave you to the desires awakened in your flesh. From a spiritual standpoint, sleeping around will bond you to a lust (sex) that will keep you in sin (2 Peter 2:19). That's not freedom.

6   How do I find a sexually compatible mate?

Answer: Marry and then teach each other. Compatibility is more often learned than found. With few exceptions, everyone is capable of learning how to satisfy their mate. First Corinthians 7:33, 34 make it clear that married people care about how to please their mate. This is more than just making them happy with gifts, loving words, and acts of kindness. It also includes satisfying their physical needs.

7   What is wrong with trying out different sex partners?

Answer: First, if you are a born-again Christian, you are part of the body of Christ, and you are disrespecting that body (1 Corinthians 6:15). You are expected to marry and be true to one person. Moreover, if you sleep around, you may become sexually comfortable with someone who will never marry you and/or addicted to having a variety of partners (Read Hosea).

8   So, how can my date and I become sexually compatible?

Answer: In the godly sense, you are not supposed to. You are not married. However, many won't wait until marriage. Those have to experiment and try different things, just as they would after marriage.

9   What's wrong with sex before marriage?

Answer: The greatest harm is to your relationship with God. Sin damages that relationship (Psalms 66:18). Your body is God's temple, and if you defile it, you may be destroyed (1 Corinthians 3:16, 17). In addition, there are physical dangers of disease, unwanted pregnancy, and becoming sexually bonded to the wrong person (1 Corinthians

6:16). That means you may remain with the wrong person simply because the sex is good. This may open you to being used by that person. Finally, sex is like taking crack, a one-hit addiction. Once you do it, it is difficult not to do it again. In Genesis 3:16, Eve is told she will give birth in pain, yet she will desire her husband. Isn't that true today? Unwanted children and painful childbirth do not keep us from seeking sexual pleasure.

10 Can pre-marital sex reduce your chances of getting married?

Answer: Yes. Women in the current age experience this truth. There are growing numbers of women who have spent years, even decades, with men who resist marriage. Why should these men marry? They are already reaping the benefits. Some consider a woman's virtue her natural dowry. That a woman has allowed pre-marital sex may diminish her in the eye of a man, even if the pre-marital sex was with him. Her weakness is a concern for men with adequacy issues – always fearing she may be weak with someone else. The virgin is still preferred because she demonstrates noble character, and she gives her husband no one else to be compared to. Proverbs 12:4 says, "A wife of noble character is her husband's crown, but a disgraceful wife is like decay in his bones. Nobility – high moral principles and ideals – will win a man. It is still true that men are treated like heroes for their sexual conquests and women like a used car if they have multiple partners. An old 1970s expression was, "Some girls are apartments, and some are homes." The big difference is that the apartment will be rented (used), the home will be bought (married).

11 Can pre-marital sex hurt your marriage?

Answer: Yes. The things you experienced with a previous lover may surface in the marriage bed. It may make sexual compatibility difficult. Compatibility means operating in harmony. However, what works with a previous lover may not work with the husband. And it might be a bone of contention. Remember what is said about a disgraceful wife in Proverbs 12:4. She is like decay in his bones. If pre-marital sex makes sexual compatibility difficult, or worse, leads to infidelity, consider that decay in his/her bones. The worst part is that the spouse may never know what the cause of the incompatibility is. Few will say I prefer the way my other lover did it.

12 How do we know when it's love?

Answer: The Apostle Paul gave a good laundry list of the characteristics of real love in 1 Corinthians 13:4-8.   Those characteristics can be used to evaluate any relationship:

1. Patience (V4) – One who truly loves you will be patient with you. Impatience often indicates selfishness – they want what they want when they want it.

2. Kindness (V4) – Those in love seek to do what is good for the other, even if it means sacrificing something.

3. No envy toward each other (V4) – True love celebrates each other's successes and never feels upstaged. Things like one earning more than the other will never be an issue. Sadly, the world teaches men that they must be the breadwinner to be truly a man. Find that in the Bible. What you will find in the Bible is the virtuous woman who deals in land development (Proverbs 31:16). Perhaps that is why the Proverb says her husband will have no lack of gain (Proverbs 31:11).

4. Praise (V4) – One who loves takes pride in the other's achievements and expresses it.

5. Serving (V4) – Love is willing to serve. However, one should never test the love of the other by requiring them to perform some service. Service should be given, not required.

6. Respect (V5) – The one who loves you is always considerate of your view, your concerns, and your needs, especially the spiritual needs.

7. They do not insist on having their way (V5) - The one who loves you will never walk over you. They won't have a problem recognizing when you have a better idea.

8. They do not hold onto anger (V5) – This does not mean they don't get angry. They are human. However, they don't let the sun go down on their anger (Ephesians 4:26).

9. Forgiving (V5) – Love covers a multitude of sins (1 Peter 4:8). The one who loves you will forgive the bad and remember the good.

10. Truthfulness (V6) – Truthfulness is the ultimate expression of trust and love. Love compels them to tell you the truth, even if it is painful, embarrassing, or might cause a momentary separation. They will also tell you a painful truth for your welfare (Proverbs 27:6).

11. They are protective (V7) – They will give themselves for you as Christ gave himself for the church (Ephesians 5:25). If you don't remember, Christ died for the church.

12. They give you their trust (V7) – The person who loves you gives you their trust. Don't betray that trust.

13. Their love is unchanging (V8) – No matter what happens in your relationship, their love remains. It is like the love of Christ.

The more of these you answer yes to, the more likely it is you've found true love.

PART 2
MARRIAGE

1   What is the purpose of marriage?

Before getting into godly answers, write what you think are some good reasons, then compare your answer to God's reasons.

1. _____.

2. _____.

3. _____.

4. _____.

5. _____.

6. _____.

7. _____.

2   What are the scriptural reasons for marriage?

Answers:

1. Companionship – God said it was not good for man to be alone. God also wanted man to have a helper that is suitable for him (Genesis 2:18).

2. Completeness – God made woman from a part of man. In uniting them, he restored man's missing part and made him even better than he was. Adam understood Eve to be bone of his bone and flesh of his flesh. In other words, the missing part of himself (Gen 2:22, 23). God also made them one in spirit (Malachi 2:15).

3. To form a new family unit (Genesis 2:24). God required a man to leave the home of his parents and establish a new home with his wife.

4. For the procreation of mankind. God ordered Adam and Eve to be fruitful and multiply (Genesis 1:28).

5. For the sanctification of children. Children brought up in a godly home with married parents are sanctified (Malachi 2:15 and 1 Corinthians 7:14). Sanctification suggests they live under godly influences and not worldly. The marriage itself is an act of obedience to the will of God. And it sets the godly example for the children to follow. Being raised in an ungodly household negatively affects the next generation. Consider how many single mothers are the children of single mothers and how many absent fathers are the sons of absent fathers.

There are other reasons for marriage, for instance, providing a social unit that can see to the care and education of children. But, the five given are probably among the most important.

BASICS OF MARRIAGE

1   What is the Biblical description of marriage?

Answer: Marriage is a covenant (solemn oath) of devotion between a man and a woman. God refers to the "wife of your covenant" in Malachi 2:14. Adam's words concerning Eve were a covenant in which he declared their eternal connection to one another – declaring her bone of his bone and flesh of his flesh. And he renamed her according to his own name – the name woman coming from man (Genesis 2:23i).

2   How serious is marriage to God?

Answer: In the Old Testament, marriage was so serious that violation of the marriage covenant was punishable by death (Leviticus 20:10). That's serious business. Two of the Ten Commandments serve to protect marriage – the seventh against adultery and the tenth commandment against coveting, which specifically mentions the neighbor's wife (Exodus 12: 14 and 17). And it remains serious in the New Testament, where marriage is described as honorable and the marriage bed undefiled, but whoremongers and adulterers will be judged (Hebrews 13:4). Judgment means the lake of fire.

3   What are common reasons for getting married?

Answers:

Because everybody is doing it – It would be great if everyone were doing it. Sadly, fewer people are looking to get married.

Because time is running out - We are instructed to wait on the Lord (Psalms 27:14). Wouldn't it hurt if you rush into a marriage and then miss the one God intended for you?

Because I want to have sex – Paul advises that if you can't resist your need for sex, you should marry (1 Corinthians 7:9). But that doesn't mean pick anybody.

Because I want to have children – One of God's conditions for bringing children into the world is that they be brought into a sanctified home (Malachi 2:15). That means married and God-fearing parents.

Because I don't want to be alone – That was God's reason for creating Eve – that Adam would not be alone (Genesis 2:18). Again, don't rush into it.

Because we are in love – What better reason than that your souls have already become knit together. Love is the best reason of all. If you do anything, do it for love (1 Corinthians 16:14).

4   How long should you know someone before getting married?

Answer: Scripture sets no time limit for it. It does show what a lack of knowledge about your mate can do. Samson suffered in part because he did not know his Philistine wife (Judges 16:4-21). It appears from successful marriages in scripture that couples were first believers in the one true God. Then, they shared a common set of beliefs about marriage and their roles in it (Genesis 28:6). It would seem from this that waiting until you know you share similar beliefs is advised. The importance of sharing cultural and religious beliefs is why Jacob told his son, Isaac, not to marry a Canaanite woman (Genesis 28:1).

LET'S TALK MARRIAGE:

1. Why do we need marriage?

Answer: First, because it was God's command (Genesis 2:18-24). Unfortunately, because God said so is not enough for many. There is another reason: an all-knowing God knew what was best for us. Sex within marriage is the best plan for mankind and society, and the only way acceptable to God. Many of the current ailments of society are connected to the destruction of the family unit.

2. What if we don't want to marry?

Answer: That is totally acceptable to God, especially if you want to dedicate yourself fully to serving Him (1 Corinthians 7:31, 32). But, if you want to have sex, you must marry so as not to sin.

3. Why is marriage losing popularity?

Answer: Because it is not what mankind wants to do – simple as that. In the spiritual sense, it is not what Satan would have mankind do as he wants us to experience eternal damnation with him. Mankind has been violating God's laws about marriage since the beginning of creation. When Cain's great, great, great-grandson Lamech took two wives (Genesis 4:19), he was wrong. When false teachers in Paul's day forbade people from marrying (1 Timothy 4:3), they were wrong. Were it not essential to a society, God would not have required it.

4 Why is there so much adultery in marriage today?

Answer: The increase in adultery results from spouses not respecting the seriousness of their marriage vows and not teaching their children to respect them. We allow our children to date and have sex with many and expect them to shut off their desire for variety on their wedding day.   Plus, society no longer has dire consequences for adultery. There is no longer a death penalty for adulterers; thus, people feel that married people are fair game. And the adulterer rationalizes that "you can't help who you love."

5 Why do so many marriages end in divorce?

Answer: Marriages fail today because people are not being raised to respect marriage (Proverbs 22:6), and they don't know the godly principles that will keep the marriage going. In fact, much of what they learn about marriage has to do with divorce – such as, "get a prenuptial."

6 Isn't marriage obsolete?

Answer: No. This is just one excuse offered by those who do not want to commit to marriage. There is nothing better for the family or society than strong marriages. Moreover, God has made it clear that marriage is honorable, but sexual relationships outside of marriage will be judged, and those who do them will not enter his kingdom (Hebrews 13:4, 1 Corinthians 6:9, 10).

7   What's wrong with shacking up?

Answer: It violates God's command. And there are consequences for that. There are couples who have shacked up for decades. Why? Only they know. They could have been married. Without marriage, they will not make it into the kingdom of God (1 Corinthians 6:9). Plus, their mates can just walk away.

8   Won't God accept a committed relationship?

Answer: Marriage is the only committed relationship God recognizes. God refers to a marriage "covenant" (Malachi 2:14). And this covenant is a serious, lifelong commitment before God. The things we call committed relationships simply aren't, as there are no vows to honor. Plus, how committed is the relationship when either partner can just walk away?

9   When we get married, isn't my body still my own to do with as I please?

Answer: No. When you marry, you own each other (1 Corinthians 7:4). You are considered one body (Genesis 2:24). The idea that the spouse's body is their own causes all manner of selfish behavior damaging to marriage.

10   Can people of the same gender marry?

Answer: With God, no. However, anything that can be passed into law can be done in the world, and same-gender marriage is now law. Mankind sees all that it does as correct (Proverbs 12:15, 16:2). However, God made them male and female (Genesis 1:27), and marriage was the institution wherein He expected love to bond them and lead to sex and the blessing of children (Genesis 1:28).

11   Why would God be against gay marriage?

Answer: Because God had defined same-gender sex as sin (Leviticus 18:22). And the Old Testament judgment for it was death (Leviticus 20:13). It would not make sense for God to bless gay marriage, which would logically lock the couple in sexual sin. As Jesus notes, from the beginning, God made them male and female (Matthew 19:4). And based on that first man-woman model, God established the marriage institution (Genesis 2:24).

12   Wouldn't marriage make gay sex acceptable?

Answer: No. If that were so, God would have given laws to that effect. He did not. Same-gender sex is called detestable in Leviticus 18:22 and unnatural in Romans 1:26, 27. And it is distinguished from fornication, which is sex outside of marriage.

13   Won't pre-marital sex show you if you are compatible enough to marry?

Answer: No. If that was true, don't you think God would have recommended that? God defines such activity as sexually immoral. And those who continue in it will not inherit the Kingdom of God (1 Corinthians 6:9, Ephesians 5:5). Sadly, many of the world's most visible role models are people living together in sin. Consider this, many that are sexually compatible divorce because they were not suited for marriage.

14   How serious must we be about marriage?

Answer: How serious we are about marriage should be guided by how serious God is about marriage. It is serious enough that God made "you shall not commit adultery" a commandment (Exodus 20:14). It was serious enough that the Law of Moses required adulterers to be stoned to death (Leviticus 20:10I). It is serious enough that a husband is expected to mercilessly rain blows on the head of the man who has touched his wife (Proverbs 6:33-35). Is that serious enough for you?

15 In the New Testament, an adulterous woman was not stoned. Doesn't that mean it is no longer a serious matter?

Answer: No. It means this is the age of grace and not the Law. In this age, the seriousness of God about adultery is evident in His promise that if you continue to do it, you won't spend eternity with Him; you will spend it in a place of pain (Revelation 21:18, 22:14,15). The believer receives grace. The woman found in adultery believed. Grace came to her when Jesus said, "Now, go and sin no more." (John 8:11).

About Salvation – Once an individual has salvation, it is sealed by the Holy Spirit of God. It is granted because that person has turned away from their sins (repented) and believed that Jesus Christ lived, died for their sins, and was resurrected (brought back to life) and now sits at the right hand of God, the Father. However, some will say they believe but do not, and Christ indicates that many will delude themselves into believing they are saved and only discover the truth when they come before the judgment seat, and he says, "I never knew you." (Matthew 7:21-23). So, what happens if you believe and then sin? Scripture is clear on this. If you confess your sins to God, he is faithful to forgive them and cleanse you (1 John 1:9). But, didn't he say that those who do such things will not inherit the Kingdom? Isn't that a contradiction? No, because he extends grace to believers. It is the difference between how your child is treated and how a stranger's child is treated. Those who accept Jesus are adopted into the family of God (Ephesians 1:5). When the unsaved disrespect God, they are simply staying on the road to damnation.

God chastises the saved because they are now His children (Hebrews 12:6, 7), but he will not renege on his promise that they will be in His

Kingdom. So, why doesn't the backslider lose his salvation? For Jesus, death has already paid for the grace of God on the believer (Romans 5:21, 6:1, 2). Thus, they only deal with the consequences/chastening here on earth. But, be forewarned. Your body is the temple of the Holy Spirit, and if you defile it, there may be dire consequences (1 Corinthians 3:16, 17). When our children act up in public, we often tell them to come home. If God sees that you are increasing in your sinful behavior, He may call you home to save you from the evil to come (Isaiah 57:1).

16   What is the sexual responsibility of the husband to the wife?

Answer: To satisfy her (1 Corinthians 7:3). That's not just New Testament speaking. God felt that making one's wife happy was so important that in His Old Testament law, he says that men should be exempt from military and other duties for the first year of their marriage specifically so as to "...bring happiness to the wife he has married." (Deuteronomy 24:5).

17   Is the husband's body his to do with as he pleases?

Answer: No. It also belongs to the wife (1 Corinthians 7:4). It is not to be given to another or denied to the wife (Exodus 20:14, 1 Corinthians 7:5).

18   When a husband cheats, isn't he just being a man?

Answer: No. Men who misuse their bodies in adultery often say, "I'm just being a man." Wrong! Real men honor their wives and marriages by remembering that their body is the property of their wife, as well as the temple of the Holy Spirit of God. They will not misuse it.

19 What is the sexual responsibility of the wife to the husband?

Answer: To satisfy him. Importantly, she should never deprive him so that he is tempted to sin (1 Corinthians 7:3, 5).

20 Is the wife's body her own to do with as she pleases?

Answer: No. It also belongs to the husband (1 Corinthians 7:4). The problem is that society has taught that it is hers alone. A common argument for abortion is that "Your body is yours." It is your decision if you want to have the baby or not. God disagrees. All mankind belongs to God, and the married couples are mutual possessions of each other.

DIVORCE

1 Should one divorce if the marriage is not working?

Answer: Jesus gives but one legitimate justification for divorce, and that one is adultery (Matthew 19:9). This also includes lack of chastity. If a man finds his wife, who claimed to be a virgin, had sexual relations before the marriage, he can divorce her. But God says he hates divorce (Malachi 2:15).

2 Do we have to divorce the spouse who cheats?

Answer: No. God allows you to choose between divorce and forgiveness. Often, forgiveness is the better course. How often do divorcees look back and wish they had not been so hasty? However, God does not expect you to be a fool. If the person is a serial cheater, divorce is probably called for.

3   What if you are unhappy in the marriage and have exhausted all remedies. Can you divorce then?

Answer: Again, God hates divorce (Malachi 2:16). We often say we've exhausted all remedies but truthfully have not. God sees through this. Our selfish desire to be free of the spouse, pursue someone else, or to return to the freedom of a single life often causes us to exaggerate about how hard we tried. The truth is, often, we've been trying to find an excuse to get out of the marriage and not reasons to stay in. God will consider one who divorces for illegitimate reasons an adulterer (Matthew 5:31, 32).

4   Does everyone have one person they should marry?

Answer: No. God can bring you someone particularly suited to you, but He has many in reserve. Abraham had a second wife after Sarah died (Genesis 25:1), and scriptures speak to conditions for remarriage (Romans 7:3).

5   If my spouse is abusive to me and/or my children, can I divorce?

Answer: There is no clear answer in scripture. However, Paul indicates that the unbeliever can leave a marriage (1 Corinthians 7:15). Most of God's advice to Christians bound in marriage shows them how to love one another and their children. However, if there is a period of separation between believers, it must happen with an eye toward reconciliation (1 Corinthian 7:10-11).

PART 3
SEX

PURPOSE OF SEX (YOUR IDEA)

Before getting into the basics of sex from a godly perspective, make a list of what you believe the purposes of sex are:

1. _____.

2. _____.

3. _____.

4. _____.

5. _____.

6. _____.

7. _____.

BASICS OF SEX (BIBLICAL)

1 What does the Bible have to say about Sex?

Answer: Plenty. The Old Testament tells us who we can and can't have sex with in Leviticus 18. Paul gives us a great summary of the importance of sex in a marriage in 1 Corinthians 7. Clearly, God intends for us to have and enjoy sex. However, He expects us to enjoy sex in the context of a marriage. And that restriction is our biggest problem. We want to have lots of sex outside of marriage and often with lots of people.

2 Is Sex a good thing?

Answer: Sex is a great thing. God gave us sex for both pleasure and procreation; in fact, the pleasure part is what keeps us procreating. When Sarah was told she would have a child after her menopause, she laughed and said, "Now that I am old and worn out, can I still enjoy sex?" (Genesis 18:12 - Good News Bible).

3 What is Sex to God?

Answer: First and foremost, it is the physical part of oneness in the marriage (Genesis 2:24, 1 Corinthians 16:16, 17). God makes us one in both body and spirit (Malachi 2:15). Sex is, of course, the way mankind is supposed to reproduce. Sex can also be the ultimate expression of love, but not always. Sometimes, one party is pretending to love the other to satisfy their lust. Sometimes, lust is being mistaken for love (2 Samuel 13:1-16). One of the ways God guards against us being deceived is through the requirement of marriage. When that person who just wants to get in your pants hears that marriage must happen first, they will think, "It ain't worth all that," and move on.

4 Isn't sex for pleasure?

Answer: Of course, it is (Proverbs 5:18, 1 Corinthians 7:3-5). God meant it to be pleasurable to encourage us to do it so that children will be born and as a way of bonding us in our marriages. Eve was told that she would suffer greater pain in childbirth because of her sin, but God also told her, "In spite of this, you will still have desire for your husband." (Genesis 3:16 Good News Bible). And isn't that how it is, even outside of marriage? We see women having multiple children for a man who, in some cases, is not good for or to them. Yet, she is driven to continue having sex with him.

The Gnostic view of sexual pleasure is that it is sinful. Nothing could be further from the truth. Sex is not a sin - having it outside of marriage is the sin. In fact, in 1 Corinthians 7, there is instruction to the couples to NOT deny each other this pleasure. God wants you to enjoy good sex. God designed us so that we could enjoy good sex. The Song of Solomon talks about good sex. But, you are only to enjoy sex within marriage. That is his only limitation.

5 Is it such a bad thing to think about having sex with someone you're not married to?

Answer: Jesus said, "But I tell you that anyone who looks at a woman lustfully has already committed adultery with her in his heart."

(Matthews 5:28). The same is true of all improper sexual thought. The first step toward sin is thinking about it. However, sexual thought toward a spouse is not sin.

6   Will sex draw us closer?

Answer: Of course, it will – if you let it. Whether in a sinful relationship or marriage, good sex is an unquestionable bonding agent. Many bad relationships endure because the sex is good. Many adulterous affairs persist because the sex is good. But God meant for good sex to bond the married couple. When married couples fail to have good sex, it is because they don't work at it. Maybe there is a medical issue that needs to be addressed, or one party wants an excuse to leave the marriage. Whatever it is, the couple must address the problem and learn what their mate desires.

7   Why does God want us to make babies?

Answer: To create new souls for Him. That is what the sex drive is all about. And bringing them up in a godly household increases their chances of seeking God.

SEX IN PRACTICE:

God has given mankind a host of rules governing sex. We ignore most of them. We behave as if we don't know that the inability to repent of sexual immorality (fornication) and adultery can keep one out of God's Kingdom (Galatians 5:19-21).

1 When is the right time to begin having sex?

Answer: When you're married, and only when you're married. Scripture says that if you can't resist the temptation to have sex, get married (1 Corinthians 7:9). Sex outside the marriage covenant is sin (1 Corinthians 6:13, 18, 7:2).

2 Can you have sex if you're engaged?

Answer: No. Engagements can be broken. If you've given in to your lust, you've lost your virginity forever, which may pose a problem for the one God meant for you to marry. Plus, engagement can be a ploy (Ephesians 5:3-7). You can only know it is serious when the marriage takes place.

3 How do I know if I'm having sex with the right person?

Answer: You're married to them. In God's eyes, the only right person for sex is the one you are married to (1 Corinthians 6:13, 7:9). So, take your time and choose wisely. The TV shows us these warm scenes where a mother looks at her daughter, hugs her lovingly, and says, "You'll just know." That mother is teaching that child sin. What parents should be telling their children is how to prepare to consummate the marriage and offer a gift that can only be given once – their virginity, innocence, and purity. It also gives the special security that comes with being the only one. Jealousy is often a matter of comparison. "Were they better?" and "What did they do that I couldn't" are the kind of questions that cause great conflict. Look at the conflict between Sarai and Hagar (Genesis 16:3, 4).

4 What if we're in a committed relationship?

Answer: Stop fooling yourself. The only committed relationship is marriage. In this day and age, couples fool themselves by living together in what they call "committed relationships." They often find out that it was all a lie when one of the committed partners cheats, or worse, leaves the relationship.

5 What about if we have safe sex?

Answer: When we hear 'safe sex,' we think of avoiding pregnancy and sexually transmitted diseases. We forget that God deals in the spiritual. If, like God, we include spiritual safety – the ability to get into the Kingdom of God – then the only safe sex is in marriage. So-called 'safe sex' is not safe and comes with both physical and spiritual consequences. By the way, many efforts at avoiding physical consequences fail.

Let's set the record straight. Women have gotten pregnant while on birth control pills. Condoms have burst or rolled down, allowing impregnation and transmission of disease. And the alteration of the condoms by heat and friction has rendered them unable to prevent the passing of the microscopic AIDS virus. So, do you really think there is such a thing as safe sex?

6 How do you get your boy or girlfriend to abstain from sex with you?

Answer: You can't force that to happen. There is a greater chance they will convince you to sin than you will convince them to abstain. That is one of the reasons the Apostle Paul encourages us to marry rather than burn with lust (1 Corinthians 7:9). But, if you're lucky enough to find someone who won't continue pressing you to have sex, you are truly blessed. Such a person allows you time to consider them as a spouse.

7 What about oral sex?

Answer: It's still sex. Oral sex is a substitute form of sex that, while it may allow us pleasure without the fear of pregnancy, it is not without its dangers. First of all, there is a bonding issue. The two may grow close, as they would with regular intercourse. This is something that should only happen in marriage. Moreover, the look, smells, and feelings will strongly tempt you to have regular intercourse. Finally, you can pass diseases orally.

8 Is oral sex sodomy?

Answer: Yes. Sodomy comes from the story of Sodom and Gomorrah, which was destroyed by God for its sinfulness. The sin illustrated in the account of the men's behavior toward the angels of God (Genesis 19) was that of lying with a man as with a woman. Oral sex is the most common way people of the same gender have sex.

9   But, is oral sex wrong?

Answer: There is no scripture against oral sex between a man and a woman. Some scholars believe the Song of Solomon contains passages that refer to oral sex (see 2:3, 2:16, 4:16, 7:2, 8:2); this is a matter of interpretation. So, the best guidance is that if it feels like a sin to you, don't do it (Romans 14:22 23).

10   What damage could a little sexual variety before marriage do?

Answer: Besides being wrong in the eyes of God, there is disease, unplanned children, and inappropriate physical bonding (1 Corinthians 6:16). The women have an added concern – being "busted out." This is a slang term meaning to have her vagina enlarged. Childbirth, frequent sex with a well-endowed man, or sexual activity with oversized instruments can enlarge and damage a woman's vagina. That can make having satisfying sex with a less well-endowed man difficult to impossible.

11   Can't we have sex if we're in love?

Answer: Only if you are also married. "You can't choose who you love" is another common excuse given for pre-marital sex and adultery. Be very clear about this – God will not forgive a sin because you were in love. Everyone should respect marriage and keep their marriage bed pure because God will judge (punish) the adulterer and the sexually immoral (Hebrews 13:4).

Don't let the words "I love you" make you do something stupid. Some people use sex to get love, and some claim to be in love to get sex. Another old saying that should be written down.

68

12 What if I save it and then find out the sex isn't good?

Answer: The first attempts at sex are rarely good. The first time is often painful for the girl. The boy might be too nervous to get an erection or too excited to last long enough to satisfy his wife. For new, inexperienced partners, there will be some learning and patience required. Give it time and put your egos aside. Listen to each other, and don't take criticism personally. Unless one of you has some serious physical problems, you'll learn to satisfy each other.

12 What if my spouse is the reason I'm not satisfied?

Answer: Don't make the mistake of accusing your mate of being at fault. It is rarely one person's fault. While saying your spouse doesn't know what to do, it may never cross your mind that you needed to tell them what to do. If one is not asking and the other is not saying, the failure is shared.

13 What is the benefit of saving yourself for marriage?

Answer: Several, to include:

1. Your obedience will preserve your relationship with God.
2. You avoid consequences like disease and unplanned pregnancy.
3. You give your spouse greater security. There are no real or perceived concerns with how they compare with the last lover when there WAS no last lover.
4. You go into marriage fully prepared to explore what is pleasurable. The person who has slept around may be

limited by their past experiences and not willing to explore and find what works with their spouse.

5. It keeps all of your sexual memories within your marriage. You can reminisce about the first time, laugh about your initial failings and recount all of your romantic mileposts. However, you normally can't discuss and enjoy those memories if your spouse was not part of them.

14 What if I've already had pre-marital sex?

Answer:

1. Confess your sin to God. He already knows about it, but you confess and repent so that He may forgive you (1 John 1:9).

2. Don't commit that sin again (Matthews 3:2, 4:17). After telling people their sins had been forgiven, Jesus would say, "Sin no more." (John 5:14, 8:11).

3. Stay away from temptation. If you are to avoid doing it again, run from situations where it might happen (2 Timothy 2:22).

4. Don't consider slipping and committing that sin again (backsliding) a death sentence. Sometimes, we falter and do what we swore we would not do. When that happens, it does not mean you've lost your salvation. The saved do sin (1 John 1:9). However, if you sin habitually, you need to question the truth of your salvation. You can't con God by just saying the words.

5. Unless a potential spouse says they don't want to know about your past, be prepared to confess to him/her your past lovers. The world will tell you that this is the absolute worst thing to do and that it is only your business, but you would be lying by omission if you did not confess this to your potential spouse. Moreover, you don't want your sexual past to blindside your spouse by either a past lover showing up or for it to become apparent in the bedroom or the medical office. The fact that a woman has lost her virginity can

become apparent in the first sexual act of marriage. In fact, in the Old Testament, a husband could challenge the virginity of his wife by simply noting she did not bleed as is expected when the hymen is ruptured for the first time (Deuteronomy 22:1-21). The wedding night is not the time for confession.

15   What about sexuality (heterosexual, homosexual, bisexual …)?

Answer: The concept of sexuality is a creation of men. We have categorized ourselves by which gender(s) we are sexually attracted to. Heterosexuality means we're attracted to the opposite gender. Homosexuality means we're attracted to the same gender.

Bisexual means we're attracted to both genders. And as time passes, more categories will be created.

16   Which sexual attractions does God accept?

Answer: The better question is what sexual behavior God accepts. He knows all of our temptations, but He only accepts heterosexual sex. God created us male and female (Genesis 1:27). He did not classify us by our sexual attractions but by the role we are designed to play in creating new life.

17   Doesn't the homosexual's body behave differently from the heterosexuals?

Answer: Only if it is conditioned to do so. Regardless of one's sexuality, our body attempts to perform its God-given procreative function. The excited male prepares to discharge the semen that can create new life. The excited female's body prepares to be penetrated and receive semen. In fact, during orgasm, a woman's body takes action to maximize the chances of pregnancy by causing the opening of the uterus to dip into the well at the end of the vagina where semen collects. No logic changes these facts.

18   What's wrong with being gay?

Answer: It can separate you from God, and the reason is simple – it is a rejection of the purposes for which God created you. It is also a rejection of his marriage model. He designed us so that we could accomplish his first instruction to us, to have children (Genesis 1:28). From the beginning on, God has instructed men and women in the roles and responsibilities of their gender. We have rejected His ideas and followed our own, which are driven by our sexual desires. God has labeled sex between two men or two women as unnatural (Romans 1:25, 26). Unbelievers and corrupt governments are free to legitimize even those things God is against. Thus, society can demand you believe there is nothing wrong with being homosexual, and that creates conflict between society and God.

19   Didn't God make people gay?

Answer: No, He didn't. God made the first man and woman and built into them the way to reproduce as well as the sexual attractions that would make that happen. Sin, however, has corrupted their descendants, both spiritually, physically, and mentally/emotionally. James, the brother of Jesus, warns us about blaming God for our temptations (James 1:13). God would not make it so that you have no choice but to sin and then punish you for the sin.

20   Well, isn't gay sex right if it feels right to me?

Answer: No, God has clearly defined homosexual and lesbian sexual lust as unnatural (Romans 1:26, 27), and He has warned us that mankind thinks everything they do is right (Proverbs 21:2). That's because we base it on the most unreliable indicator – how it feels and how we feel about it.

21   What's the difference between being Black or White and being hetero or homosexual?

Answer: Black and white are physical attributes.   Hetero and homosexual are sexual attractions. They have nothing in common, although there are attempts to link them.

22   So, why are people gay?

Answer: There are numerous theories given from genetics to social influences.   However, Roman 1:18-27 suggests that God has given them over to this lust because they rejected Him and His truths.

23   Aren't people who are against homosexuality just hateful?

Answer: Some act out of hate; some act out of love. The confusion comes when the hateful quote the Bible.   Real Christians act out of love. It is as simple as this – the people who hate gays are personally offended by homosexuality and show that hate toward the gay. The person who loves you does not want you to engage in activity that will eternally separate you from God. They would be equally concerned with any other activity that would keep you out of God's kingdom (1 Corinthians 6:9). However, they can relate to gays in every respect, except one; they can't accept the sexual activity.

24   Shouldn't education make people more accepting of gay sex?

Answer: No.   The false claim, "They're just uneducated," is an arrogant suggestion that those who see gay sex as sin are somehow less knowledgeable. They are often very knowledgeable on the matter but simply disagree as to whether or not it constitutes a sin.   Some define educated as indoctrinated. You can't be politically correct and a Christian. God is not politically correct. He makes the rules concerning sin, and Christians true to God's word see same-gender sex as sin, based on God's word.

25 Isn't rejecting a gay person's romantic advances sinful judging?

Answer: It depends on what you mean by judging. If someone is acting like they have the authority to pronounce judgment according to their own standards, they are in the wrong (Matthew 7:1). However, if they reject sexual advances of any kind because they see it as sin, they are not judging. They are replying in accordance with scripture. They are replying truthfully. It is not judgment just because it is not what you want to hear. It is the same as rejecting adultery, incest, or other sexual sins.

26 How should Christians respond to the sexual advances of someone who is gay?

Answer: As they would anyone who makes sinful sexual advances. Politely refuse them.

27 What if I love my gay lover?

Answer: God's laws have but one love exception, and that is that God loved us so much that he sacrificed his only Son to pay for our sins (John 3:16). Other than that, God's laws are against sinful acts. And in all of scripture, God does not forgive any sin because of the emotions connected to it. In the Old Testament, God calls for stoning. Nowhere in the Law of Moses did he say, except if they are in love.

28 What if I'm gay and at peace with that?

Answer: Scripture would indicate that God has given you over to a reprobate mind (Romans 1:28). In other words, He has seen that you will not let go of this and, therefore, rejected you (Jeremiah 6:30). What you call 'peace of mind' is a lack of conscience concerning being gay.

29 But Jesus didn't say anything against homosexuality, did he?

Answer: As said in an earlier section, there is one of two answers – yes, and we don't know. Scripture says that Jesus is the word of God (John 1:1); thus, the words given in Leviticus were from the pre-incarnate Jesus. Paul indicates that he received his words from Christ (Galatia 1:11, 12). Finally, Christ did much more than was recorded (John 21:25). That may include comments on homosexuality. Finally, Jesus said there would be no change to the law until earth passes away (Matthew 5:18). That includes laws concerning homosexuality found in Leviticus.

30 Would marrying my gay lover make our sex OK?

Answer: No. Some insist that marriage between members of the same gender will make the relationship acceptable to God. Not so. It could be considered locking the gay couple in sin. Moreover, God gave no laws allowing the marriage of two men or two women. Indeed, he gave law requiring the stoning of two men who sleep together (Leviticus 20:13).

31   Why should Christians judge me for wanting to have gay sex?

Answer: They should not judge you. Judging you is God's business (James 4:12). And he has made his position abundantly clear to us in the scriptures. They should, however, know God's position.

32   Shouldn't Christians be tolerant of Sexual issues?

Answer: No. If you tolerate a sin, it will flourish. The godly have an obligation to warn the sinner of the consequences of their sins (Ezekiel 3:18, 19). They are also expected to protect their home from ungodly influences. Take the position of Joshua – "As for me and my house, we shall serve the LORD." (Joshua 24:15).

33   How can gay sex hurt anyone?

Answer: It can separate you from God. And it replaces the bond intended to exist between man and woman with a same-gender bond that is equally strong.

34   What should I do if I am having gay sex and want to be right with God?

Answer: Confess it as a sin and resolve never to engage in it again (1 John 1:9). Prepare for hard times ahead. You will be tempted by your lust (James 1:4). You will likely always have gay desires, and yours will be a heavy cross to bear. Try to avoid tempting situations.

35   Can I be cured of homosexuality?

Answer: "Cured" is the wrong word, "delivered" from it is more appropriate. It may remain a "thorn in the side" for you. What you can expect is that God will give you the strength and grace to deal with it (2 Corinthians 12:9).

36 So, must I learn to be heterosexual to have sex?

Answer: No. What you must learn is holiness. Holiness is the opposite of sinfulness. Keep in mind that it is your spirit and not your flesh that is saved, and the two will always battle (Romans 7:23). In holiness, right and wrong are what God says is right and wrong. In worldliness, right and wrong are mostly a function of how you feel about a thing.

37 Will having sex with the opposite sex help?

Answer: No. When trying to get away from sin, practicing another sin is never the answer, nor would it help to enter into a marriage as an attempt to 'cure' one's self. A marriage should only happen if you have totally forsaken the gay sex life and you have found sex with the opposite gender truly enjoyable for you. Otherwise, you are deceiving yourself and your spouse.

38 So, what can I do about my sexuality?

Answer: Pray for God's help. Realize that your body is just the source of your sensations, but that sexual attraction is in the mind and emotions. Then, renew your mind (Romans 12:2). That means to immerse yourself in God's word and pray for the help of the Holy Spirit in changing your thinking so that it lines up with God's. Your sexual temptations won't go away, but with God's help, you can resist them.

39 Aren't I being a hypocrite by denying my gay feelings?

Answer: Yes. So, don't deny your temptations. When someone says, "You're a hypocrite. You know gay sex excites you." Reply to them, "No, I'm not. I admit my weakness. I just choose to live a Christian life."

40 What if I refuse to give up my gay sexual activities?

Answer: Enjoy this life prepared to receive the judgment due unrepentant sinners. God has made it clear that the unrighteous will not enter heaven (the Kingdom). But don't feel picked on. Practicing homosexuals are not the only unrighteous – (Read 1 Corinthians 6:9).

41 Doesn't the fact that God has not struck me down mean He condones my sexual activity?

Answer: No. When God allows you to live another day, we call that grace. We sometimes mistake His patience for approval when God is really waiting for us to change our ways (Romans 2:4). We are in the age of grace, and God wants all men to be saved (1 Timothy 2:4, 2 Peter 3:9). However, God won't put up with us forever (Psalms 103:9). If we die in our sins, He will punish us at the judgment seat.

42 What about when God blesses me? Doesn't that mean he approves of my sex life?

Answer: No. And that's true of all sins. A big mistake people make is to think God's blessings are the same as approval. God blesses the good and the bad (Matthews 5:45). Keep in mind that Paul and Barnabas warned their disciples, saying, "We must go through many hardships to enter the kingdom of God." (Acts 14:22). If you're not having any troubles, then it might mean that the trouble maker (Satan) is happy with how you're living. Keep in mind that Satan did not bring suffering on a sinful man in the book of Job. He chose to pick on a God-fearing and righteous man (Job 1:1).

43 Where is God's love for sexual sinners?

Answer: Where his love for everyone else is. He has sacrificed his only son to cover your sin (John 3:16). Now, it is up to you. Confess your sinfulness, repent, and accept Jesus Christ as your Lord and Savior or remain in your sin. And, if you believe in Jesus Christ and you want to receive his salvation, pray the following in sincerity:

Dear God. I am a sinner. I've done wrong, and I'm sorry. I am turning away from my sins, and I want to have a relationship with You. I believe that Your Son, Jesus Christ, came to earth to save me from the penalty for my sins, which is death and eternal suffering. He died on a cross to pay for my sins, and You raised Him from the dead. He now sits at Your right hand and offers me eternal life if I receive Him as my Lord. I receive Jesus as my Lord and savior right now. Thank you, Lord, for saving me – Amen.

Short Version:

Dear God, I confess and repent of my sins and make your son, Jesus, who died for my sins, the Lord of my life. Amen

PART 4
ABOUT CHILDREN

GETTING PREGNANT

1 A single person's question – How do I avoid unwanted pregnancy?

Answer: The best answer is to not have sex. But that isn't working in our society, is it? Everybody is trying to have the pleasure of sex without the natural consequences. And if you're married, that makes things even harder because you can't deny sex to your spouse.

2 What if you're married and one of you doesn't want children?

Answer: Don't deceive your spouse. For an example of how God deals with such deception, look at the story of Judah and Tamar (Genesis 38). In this time, if a man died, his brother was obliged to marry and impregnate his widow. The child she conceives would be considered the heir of the dead brother. This is called the kinsman redeemer law. When Tamar's husband Judah died, his brother Onan took her as a wife and had sex with her. But Onan didn't want her to have children he could not call his own, so he spilled his semen on the ground (Genesis 38:9). God killed him for doing that. Based on that, how do you think God would feel about someone secretly taking birth controls and deceiving the spouse into thinking they are barren

– or a husband secretly getting a vasectomy. If you disagree on the important issue, you should not get married.

3   Aren't children just a burden?

Answer: Only for those who have the idea that children get in the way of success and those who have not yet prepared themselves for parenthood. God considers children a blessing. Scripture call sons a heritage from the Lord and children a reward from the Lord (Psalms 127:3). We make a serious mistake when we see children as burdens and inconveniences.

4   Why does God want us to have children?

Answer: Each child is a new soul for God to love and an agent of God's grace. God's holy acts of deliverance for His people begin with the birth of a child that God has given special gifts (Deuteronomy 18:15, Judges 13:3, Isaiah 9:6). Indeed, God knows his plan for every child before they are born (Isaiah 49:1, Psalm 137:19, Jeremiah 1:5).

DEALING WITH UNWANTED PREGNANCY

① What if I make a mistake and get pregnant?

Answer: Have the child and learn from your error. In Jesus' words, "Sin no more." And don't feel alone. Many pregnancies are unplanned. But, the best advice for those who want to stay in God's good graces is to have the child. To do otherwise is a sin before God. You may give the child up for adoption afterward but have the child.

② Why can't I abort the child?

Answer: Abortion is a form of idol worship. You have sacrificed a life that could have served God to your own self-interests. It is similar to sacrificing the child to false gods as the intent is to gain some benefit from that god. In abortion, the benefit is the freedom to act without the responsibility of parenthood. Moreover, God considers it murder. This is made clear in the Old Testament, where God said that if an unborn child's life was lost due to induced labor, the person causing it would have to forfeit his/her life (Exodus 21:23). In light of God's command that if a man sheds blood, then, by man, shall his blood be shed (Genesis 9:6), God sees the life of the unborn as equal to that of the born. God hates hands that shed innocent blood

(Proverbs 6:16, 17). What is more innocent than an unborn child who has not had an opportunity to sin?

3   But aren't there good reasons for having an abortion?

Answer (Christian): Yes. Sometimes, pregnancy threatens the life of the mother or child. However, the overwhelming majority of those having abortions are engaged in a form of after-the-fact contraception. Understand that this is a spiritual matter for the Christian. Most of the "good" reasons for having an abortion are worldly and self-centered. "I'm just not ready for a child" is a common justification. But, no one seems to say, "...So we won't have sex until I'm ready to have a child."

4   Aren't there some common-sense reasons for abortion?

Answer: Non-religious reasons for abortion are the application of selfish reasoning to illegitimate life laws. Such reasoning often begins with convenient definitions of the unborn child and granting the mother godly power over it. Make the unborn child an inhuman parasite without rights instead of a human being in the early stages of development, then apply reasoning like that of Russian-born writer Ayn Rand. Ms. Rand says, "An embryo has no rights. Rights do not pertain to a potential, only to an actual being. A child cannot acquire any rights until it is born. The living take precedent over the not-yet-living (or the unborn)." This reasoning is understandable when you consider her system of ethics, which she calls rational egoism (rational self-interest). If you have not the Spirit of God and are worldly, then what Ms. Rand says makes sense to you, and you will follow it. But, if you are of God, you see that child as God sees that child and will not abort it.

5   Why does God require us to have children?

Answer: Childbearing is how mankind participates in God's work of creating new souls for him to love and to serve Him. And the newborn body is the training ground of that new soul.

6   What if the baby is not a "viable" baby yet?

Answer: Viable to whom? We hear that it is no crime to kill an unborn child before it is 'viable.' Viable, in the scientific sense, means it is able to live, independent of the mother. A child is viable to God even before it is conceived (Jeremiah 1:5). The world's idea of what is viable saves us from our conscience but won't save us from the wrath of God.

7   What if it is still a fetus or zygote?

Answer: Don't be confused by the language. Fetus is just another name for an unborn child that has all its parts. Zygote is the name given to that cluster of living cells that carry in them all the potential of human life. These words sound better than "baby" when discussing abortion, and that's why they are used. God said in the Old Testament that if you cause someone to abort a child, there is a penalty (Exodus 21:22). God didn't say how premature the child had to be.

8   Isn't abortion a matter of rights?

Answer: Not with God. That's how the world convinces us – it asks us to see it in a way other than how God sees it. Remember how the serpent-shaped the way Eve viewed the forbidden fruit? With respect to rights, the world sees unborn children as having no rights. God requires a life for a life when a child is aborted. He obviously sees the unborn child as having a right to live.

9   What is the bottom line on abortion?

Answer: Don't abort a child unless it is going to be stillborn. Have the living baby. You will physically recover, your child can be adopted, and you can go on with your life and not have the blood of an innocent child on your hands and conscience.

10   Will God forgive me for having an abortion?

Answer: Yes – if it occurred before you came to Christ. God will forgive anything. But, you cannot fool God. You cannot pre-plan that you're going to have an abortion and then ask for forgiveness afterward. A look at God's harsh treatment of deliberate sin in the Old Testament should indicate the plight of those who disrespect God with premeditated sin and fake plea for forgiveness (Exodus 21:14, Number 15:20, Deuteronomy 1:43, 17:11, 12). God looks for true sorrow and repentance in your heart.

RAISING A CHILD

Among the many questions submitted by teenagers for this book were a few about rearing and disciplining children. This book was not intended to address these problems. However, if it is God's will, a book on that subject will come.

www.ingramcontent.com/pod-product-compliance
Lightning Source LLC
Chambersburg PA
CBHW072207090426
42740CB00012B/2421